"Am I Going to Heaven?"

Letters from the Street

Sr. Mary Rose McGeady

Covenant House

DEDICATED
to the 1,000,000
kids who will sleep
on America's streets tonight –
scared, cold, hungry,
terrified, lonely
and desperate to find
someone who cares.

Table of Contents

Introduction

*"Sister, I just need to know
one thing...."*

She tried to lift her head up from the hospital bed pillow when I walked in, but she couldn't do it. The tears in her eyes were just too heavy. The beautiful girl I had known was just a shadow of a kid now, skin and bones rattling and hacking inside a 79-pound body.

After three long years of scratching and surviving on the streets as a street kid, Michelle had now gone to the hospital to die. She was just 17 years old.

"Sister ... Sister, I need to know something," she whispered. "Please, tell me something."

"Anything, Michelle" I said. "What do you need to know?"

"I ... want to know about Heaven," she said. "I mean...." For the longest time she looked up at the ceiling, not able to finish the sentence. It wasn't just because she was too tired to ask her question. She was also too scared. She desperately needed to know something, but she wasn't sure she'd like my answer.

"Sister, ... I ... I wonder ... I mean ... Am I going, do you think?" she finally said. "Am I going to Heaven? Even a street kid like me?" Her eyes stayed riveted to the safest place in the room, the ceiling, and then fell silently. Huge tears spilled out down her face.

I bent down and hugged her, and told her I knew God had a special place for her. I told her how much I loved her, and how much I believed in her. Even though at that moment I knew I was a poor substitute of God's love for her, I knew she appreciated my words. She cried in my arms, and whispered a 'thank you.' The next day, Michelle died in her sleep.

I can't get her out of my mind. I simply can't forget that beautiful child, and the agony on her face. I see her always, every single time I look into another kid's face.

And I see her a lot ... 1,200 times last night alone.

Hi, my name is Sr. Mary Rose McGeady and I run a crisis shelter for kids who live on America's streets. Last night more than 1,200 street kids knocked on my shelter door, desperately searching for the same things that brought Michelle to me — a hot meal, clean clothes, someone to hug them, someone to tell them they are good ... someone to care.

These kids are among the most amazing children I have ever met. Thrown away by parents who simply don't want them, or driven away by parents who abuse them, these kids (many as young as 10!) have been forced to survive on the streets by themselves. With no money. No one to lean on. No memories of ever feeling good, and loved, and wanted. Precious little hope of ever surviving.

Somehow though, many of these kids make it. In ways that will surprise you, astound you, and inspire you. In short, I think my kids — America's street kids — are the most beautiful and courageous children you will ever meet.

This book is my love story about them.

"Am I Going to Heaven?" is my story about the struggle these kids face, written from my vantage point as head of America's largest crisis shelter for children. In this book, I have chronicled a year of living and breathing with these amazing kids on the street, giving you a rarely-seen-or-heard-before inside view of what these kids do to live and survive.

Because I want you to feel, and see, and know what their lives have been like, I have told their stories chronologically — through letters I wrote to friends and supporters who share this life-saving mission with me.

I should warn you in advance that these letters about my kids are unedited, stark, and sometimes graphic, mirroring the lives these kids sometimes lead. Most important of all, these are *the kid's* stories. Told by them. From mouths that quivered in fear, and in some wonderful moments found the strength to smile and laugh.

I feel privileged God gave me the chance to be a part of it....

Sister Mary Rose McGeady
June 6, 1994

No stranger I, to death.
He lives with me each day.
He tempts me with my grave,
and hides the price I'll pay.

A poem from
a street kid.

Chapter 1

**"If they find me,
they'll kill me."**

May, 1993

"I'm what they call a mule, Sister," the girl said.

"They made me smuggle drugs for them," she said.

"They stuffed cocaine in little plastic bags, and made me swallow them," she said.

She sat in our clinic — her on the edge of a nervous breakdown, me on the edge of my seat, searching for some words that could help Liz bear a lifetime of unbearable pain.

I know what the term "mule" means on the street, but I have never met one so young.

Liz is 14 years old.

"The drug runners made me a drug mule. Me and my friend, Michelle."

"Michelle is dead now," she said. "She was the same age as me."

"That must have been awful," I said.

"It was," she said.

"Michelle and I come from London and we did the New York run. In London, they'd make us swallow bags filled with drugs. Sometimes I didn't even know what was in them.

"A few weeks ago, Michelle and I were waiting to get picked up when she started to feel real sick. She got worse and worse and then she collapsed on the sidewalk. When the dealers came to pick us up, they made me leave her there.

"I found out that she died on the way to the hospital. A bag burst inside her and the drugs killed her.

"And I'm next, Sister. Sooner or later. I know it. That's why I had to come here. But if they find me, they'll kill me."

"No one's going to kill you, Liz. You're safe here."

"You don't know these people, Sister. They wouldn't think twice about shooting you or anyone else."

For another hour, I went around and around with Liz, trying to convince her she was safe ... trying to convince her she was worth saving.

She told me about her life. How her mother needed money so she put Liz to work with a local pimp. She was 12 years old. Liz shook with disgust and pain when she told me how she was forced to have sex with dozens of perverted men every week.

Then, six months ago, her pimp decided he had a new use for her. He wanted her to carry drugs through customs — to be a drug "mule."

Liz resisted, but her pimp said it wasn't her choice. He owned her, and she had to do what he wanted.

So out of fear, Liz became a mule, part of a rapidly-growing herd of defenseless kids being manipulated and used by the multi-billion dollar drug and sex industry.

These greedy men in their $2,000 designer suits use kids like Liz to smuggle drugs for some unforgivable reasons. Because kids are trustworthy. Because they are innocent looking. In short, because they are kids.

Kids like Liz are being increasingly used to run drugs because they are the perfect "front men" for the crime ... and the best "insurance" that the deal will be completed.

One policeman I talked to recently summed it up: "These kids are the perfect puppets, Sister. They don't raise a lot of suspicion. And they're so young, and so scared, they do exactly what they're told...."

I loathe these drug dealers and pushers. I loathe and despise what they do to kids like Liz. I hate their cruelty and viciousness. I know maybe I should find a place in my heart to forgive them, God, but I can't. I just can't....

"I couldn't take it anymore," Liz said, tears gushing out. "I'm not bad, Sister. I'm really not bad...."

"I know that, Liz," I said. "I know. But, don't worry. I just know we'll be able to help." Somehow, those words made her cry even harder.

I don't know how to thank you. If it wasn't for you, Liz would have had nowhere to run. Without Covenant House, kids like Liz would be trapped forever — or they'd be dead.

I wish I were exaggerating, but I'm not. It's true.

I also wish I could tell you that Liz will be okay.

I honestly don't know. She's been so traumatized by these events that she's talked about committing suicide. We were so concerned we rushed her to St. Vincent's Hospital, for evaluation.

She's back with us now and thank God she's better. And, if human love can save her, she's in the right place ... thanks to you.

But kids like her are so badly damaged, it will take more than human love. Say a prayer for her, will you?

She is so young. Living on the streets forces kids to grow up, but it can't change the fact that Liz is just a child. A child who should be doing her homework, and wondering whether that cute older boy — you know, the *sophomore* — likes her.

Thank you for all you do for kids like Liz. We never forget that they are children of God, nor do we ignore the miraculous fact that you care for them deeply enough to help.

Dear Sister Mary Rose,

I just read Liz's story and it moved me deeply. I too was once one of your many troubled and disturbed kids.

Although I didn't stay long, I wandered into Covenant House to escape a terrifying life on the street. Because I had a drug problem and was very tired and confused and I needed to come home. You people were wonderful to me and gave me my ticket to a new life.

I have a 13-year-old daughter now. Please tell Liz I am praying for her! And please help me save my daughter from going through what I and many kids, go through as a young teenager.

M.C.

If

If all lips spoke the truth,
All pride was cast aside,
Greed was packed and stored away,
And jealousy subside.
If love could rule the universe,
Kindness was sown to every race,
Then one could glance into a mirror
And view God in his face....

Written by a 16-year-old
girl on the street

Chapter 2

*"Dying in here is better
than living outside."*

June, 1993

The trembling left hand reached out from under the hospital bed sheets, and tried to scribble a note on the pad.

He was just a skeleton boy, more bones than skin, and it hurt just to watch him. Tubes ran everywhere across the bed and along the floor, from his nose, his mouth, and his arms.

I bent over the hospital bed to read the message:

"I'm OK, Sister," the dying boy's message said.

"Let's pray."

I looked into the kid's hollow eyes and saw the tears begin to fill up every corner. I will never forget praying the Our Father with him as long as I live.

His name is Al, and this week or next, this very wonderful young kid is going to die of AIDS.

I can't stop thinking about this kid, and praying for this kid, and crying for this kid. I wish to God I were a little stronger about this, but it's really hard....

He came to us a while back, one of the first kids I ever got to meet at Covenant House. He didn't so much walk into our shelter, but charge in, a 5'7" bundle of sass and swagger bouncing inside high-top sneakers. He was loud, boastful, theatrical, innately kind and comical.

We all fell in love with him instantly.

But beneath Al's happy veneer, we had uncovered an awful truth about our new friend — he was dying.

For those first few months, Al managed to keep his secret away from a lot of the kids, although he was never able to fool us.

I can still vividly see him leaving our cafeteria, a trail of kids' laughs trailing behind him. And then I'd see him stagger to our medical clinic, and quietly beg for help. "I don't feel good ... I need to rest," he'd always say.

He'd tell the kids he had a cold, but we knew it was AIDS.

For the longest time we all wondered how a kid could be dying inside, but be so outwardly happy.

And then one day, while we were talking he told me how.

"Sister, you've gotta understand something. Dying in here is better than living outside.

"I mean, I never felt like I was alive when I was outside. I never had a father growing up, and my mother ... my mother never wanted me. I can't remember ever being hugged, ever being told I was loved, ever feeling wanted.

"Then, about two years ago, my mother abandoned me in the middle of the night, and I was homeless. I've spent the last two years on the street, knowing what it's like to be hungry, and beaten, and used, and bought and sold. Do you call that living?"

As the AIDS got worse, and his body deteriorated, Al never seemed to lose hope. Even when the AIDS grip began to eat away at his body, and some of the other kids became more reluctant to be with him (the fear of AIDS is enormous on the streets), Al kept smiling.

And he began to do one more thing. He started praying.

Even while he was physically deteriorating, Al's faith in God became stronger and stronger. In letting go and putting his trust in God, Al found a reservoir of courage within himself.

It was one of the most beautiful things I've ever seen.

I want to thank you for being with Al these last few moments. It's meant a lot to him that you've been there for him. Even though you've been miles away, I know your love and your prayers have been with him, just as much as they are for every single lost and hurting and sometimes dying homeless kid at Covenant House.

Please, say an extra prayer for Al tonight, if you can? It would mean a lot to me. I can never thank you enough for caring about our kids as you do.

God knows, we never ever stop thanking God you found us, every day.

Dear Sister Mary Rose,

Hi, my name is _____, and I'm fifteen. I read your letter about Al.

I'm very emotional when I read, or hear, or even think about the kids my age, older, and younger who live on the streets throughout the U.S. I feel a need to help them, always have. Your letter touched me deeply; I cried after reading it. I want to help, I want to give them love directly; but right now I don't have all that much to offer. Enclosed is a donation of twenty dollars (I don't have a job yet, so I don't come into money too often. I'll try to donate when I can; I know they need it.) When I get older I would like to work with Covenant House in some way or another along with my writing. Give your kids my love; I really do care.

E.L.

Dear God,
I just want someone to love me, someone to talk to
when I need to talk. Someone to cry on when I need
to cry. Most of all someone to love me and walk as
far as they wish through my life. Amen.

A prayer written
by a kid in our
Covenant House chapel

Chapter 3

"I want to go back where I belong."

July, 1993

The other kids called her "The Girl in The Hood."

She came to our shelter one frigid night, a very large and unsure girl wearing a huge red hood pulled over her head.

From the second she stepped inside, she cast a shadow over our shelter — a shadow that was bigger and shrouded in more mystery than any kid I have ever met.

"Who is that girl in the hood, anyway," the kids would whisper. "What does she look like under that hood? Does she ever take it off? *Ever?*"

"She just needs some space," I told them. "Please give her time."

For her first 30 days at Covenant House, *she never once took her hood off,* never once showed her eyes. She wore the hood every minute in the morning, and every minute throughout the day. She even wore her hood to bed at night, pulling it tightly over her eyes as she drifted off to sleep.

All our cajoling and pleading and counseling couldn't get her to take it off. She wouldn't — she couldn't — give away the one thing in life that helped her hide.

The kids found her ... unnerving. Hard to understand. A little scary. Even the toughest, street-hardened, seen-it-all-and-had-it-all-done-to-them kids kept a safe distance away.

From the beginning we decided to be extra patient with her, to give her as much space as we could. But always, always, we were there, too. Because she obviously needed us there more than any kid I ever met....

Our conversations, (and we never stopped trying to start one,) weren't much longer than a hiccup those first weeks. "Hi," I'd say. "Hi," she'd say. "I'd love to talk to you when you get a chance," I'd say. "O.K.," she'd say, as she walked away.

Many times, while she was all alone at a table by herself, I'd drop by to say hello and pat her on the back. "I'd love to talk to you when you're ready," I'd say. "O.K.," her hood would nod. "Later," she'd say.

For a month this went on, little snippets of conversation here, a nod there. Her words, so few spoken over those 30 days, always came the same way, barely a whisper, head and eyes down, escaping under the cover of her hood.

We learned that her name was Nancy. She was a runaway from North Carolina. She had been severely abused at home, by both her parents, and was so terrified she bought a bus ticket (with the only money she had) and escaped to New York. She ended up at the Port Authority, all alone, and wandered the streets for weeks ... until a kind policeman brought her to us. She was scared. And hurt. And no one cared about her. No one.

"No one wants me," she said one night out of the blue while she was getting up from dinner. She never looked up, when she said it. At that moment, it was more clear than ever why Nancy hid inside her hood. I mean, her hood was much more than an article of clothing for Nancy. It was her cocoon ... her sanctuary, the only safe and secure place that was hers and hers alone.

By hiding beneath her hood, Nancy was able to hide the incredible feelings of insecurity that paralyzed her. Her hood became her "alter ego" — her protector (the only protector she knew). Her round-the-clock security blanket. The only place in the world she felt safe.

Finally, though, our love got through to her....

"I was wondering, Nancy," I said again one day. "We really think it's time we get you some new clothes. I'd really like to buy you a new dress to wear." (It was probably the 99th time I suggested it — I wasn't really expecting much.)

The hood slowly lifted, and her eyes met mine (it was only for a split second, but it was a first). "Really?" she said. After we got her a new outfit, I brought her up to Billie, one of our super counselors who ironically had also been a hairdresser. "Will you let Billie do your hair, Nancy?" I asked. "You'd look so nice."

"I don't know," she said. "I'm so ugly," she said.

"Everyone thinks I am," she said. For the first time, I could see tears streaming down her face.

"Please let us," I said. "You'll look terrific," I said, putting my hand on her hood, and gently pulling it back.

It was difficult keeping our composure those next few moments, seeing and feeling and touching and smelling hair that had been matted down for months. Our new scissors almost failed, her hair was so stiff.

"Please stop ... maybe this isn't a good idea," she kept saying. "I'm so ugly ... don't waste your time."

"You look great," we said. "You really do."

During the next week, a very scared and unsure kid didn't leave her room that much. Every night, around 5:45, I'd see her make a quick beeline to the cafeteria, eyes straight down, and then back to her room thirty minutes later.

"Hi Nancy, it's great to see you today. You look wonderful," I would always tell her. "Thanks," she would mumble.

But as time wore on, Nancy ventured out of her room more often. Slowly, she began to talk to the other kids. To smile, and even to laugh. Her counseling sessions, once frustratingly short, became longer. The pain and anger she had literally wrapped inside her, began to flow out.

It wasn't an overnight transformation. There were days when Nancy slipped back into her own little world. But slowly, surely, she began to blossom under the light of our love, a beautiful child of God discovering an internal beauty she had never known.

She was literally reborn.

Then last week, she surprised us all. "I want to go back to North Carolina," she said. "To live near my old home. I've got a cousin who says I can live with her. She's a good person. I want to go back where I belong."

A few hours ago, I picked up the phone to hear a cheerful voice calling from North Carolina. "It's working out great, Sister," she said. "I just got a job today," she said. "It doesn't pay much, but it's a start. Thanks ... thanks," she said.

"I'm so happy," I said.

"Thank you, thank you," she said. The voice was filled with tears, but I never heard one so beautiful.

Dear Sister Mary Rose,

I was so touched by your letter about Nancy.

When I was at the age of eight my father started coming around to see us. At this time I knew nothing about the sexual abuse that he did to my older sisters. So I naturally wanted to be with him. My mother allowed this hoping that he had changed. Well, you see I thought when I slept with him and he would cover his whole body over mine and do things to me, I thought this was love. When I was 13 and knew more about the facts of life, he tried to have sex with me. He trapped me and I could not move. But by some means I escaped his grip and ran. I told my mother about it and she refused to let me go and visit him again. I wanted very much to die and end this nightmare I was living. Sister, I am now 39 years old and my life has been freed from drugs for 13 years. I am a living witness that God can save and God can deliver.

D.S.

I do not consider myself to be a follower,
just a lonely deserted soul in a barbaric city,
who walks his own treacherous path in life.

> *Written by Brian,*
> *after six months alone*
> *on the street*

Chapter 4

"You're not my kids ...
you're too expensive."

August, 1993

"I just lost my brother, Sister."

"He's only eight years old, Sister. I can't believe I lost him...."

The little girl's face was tortured with guilt and fear. Tears dripped down her face while she looked up at me. A pouring rain beat down her hair. The girl — the babysitter — the guardian — was only 13 years old.

"Come inside," I said. "What's your name?" I asked. "Please tell me what happened," I said.

"My name's Annie," she said. "My little brother's out there alone," she said, pointing outside to the 8,000,000 person city that buzzed around our building.

"Do you want me to call your parents?" I asked.

"You can't," the 13-year-old dripping kid said. "I don't have any parents. They're dead," she said.

It hurt hearing the words. Her tears began to gush out faster.

"I mean, I lived with my aunt ... but she threw me and Freddie out today. She said, 'You're not my kids ... you're too expensive ... I'm tired of taking care of you.'" Annie looked up at me and paused, giving me plenty of time to catch up. I reached down and hugged her.

"I didn't know what to do, Sister," the 13 year old said. "Me and Freddie went back to our aunt, but she wouldn't let us in. So we walked around for a long time.

"I would've gone someplace else, but we don't have anyplace to go."

"Then, about an hour ago, I turned around to talk to Freddie ... and he was gone.

"I'm really scared, Sister," she said. "He's just a little kid." The tears began flowing really fast now.

"I mean, I knew enough to find a policeman, and he brought me here. But Freddie ... he doesn't know what to do."

"He's just a little kid," she said. "He's only eight years old."

She is 13 years old, and she is hungry, and she is terrified, and she is completely alone in a city of 8,000,000 people, and she has just been literally kicked out onto a dead-end street by the only adult she knows in the whole world ... and she is worried about her little brother.

The only thing in the world she cares about right now is rescuing her little brother, Freddie.

Kids like her overwhelm me sometimes.

I mean, whenever I see a kid like her, I find myself wondering — how can she cope? How? How can she stand there and face the next moment? At her age?

What would I do in her shoes at that age? Could I have done it?

If I were totally alone — totally alone — and just 13 years old in this huge city, would I be strong enough to shelter a little brother while I was shaking inside? Would I be mature enough? Brave enough?

Would I be good enough to worry more about my little brother than about myself ... even though I was terrorized and dying inside?

If I were 13 years old and homeless, could I possibly be as strong as the little girl sleeping tonight in our shelter?

Can you imagine a child more courageous?

I am in awe of this beautiful kid. I am in absolute awe of kids like her....

As for Freddie? We're all praying very hard that he'll be found real soon, and brought to us safe and sound.

And once Freddie is safe and sound (I refuse to even think about the alternative), and we reunite him with Annie, we're then going to help find these kids a home. A good home. A place where brave and beautiful kids who care more about each other than they do about themselves, can find loving parents who care, too. These kids deserve that much. Every kid does....

P.S. IMPORTANT UPDATE ... I HAVE GREAT
NEWS! Since I started this letter to you, two
wonderful things have happened! First, Freddie's
been found — scared, trembling, terrified — but

safe nonetheless. The second thing? We've found these two beautiful kids a home. A place where they will finally find the love and encouragement every kid deserves. Thanks so much for making this story possible. Thank you! You're great!

Dear Sister Mary Rose,

My name is _____ and I'm 30 years old.

When I was 17 I was homeless too, so I don't have to read about it, I've been through it just like those kids you've written about. It's a terrifying feeling to be out there in the world lost and cold and hungry and people look at you as if you aren't even human. My Mother passed away when I was only 17 and my sisters and I had no way to pay the rent, so we all just drifted apart. It's hard to look on the bright side when all you see is darkness and it's hard to walk towards the light when no one is there to reach out for you. You just have to do whatever it takes to survive out there. There is hope, there is a light at the end of the tunnel. I know....

Please, please tell your kids that all is not lost!

B.C.

Learn to Listen

Learn to listen like a teddy bear,
With ears open and mouth closed tight.
Learn to forgive like a teddy bear,
With an open heart, not caring who is right.
Learn to love like a teddy bear,
With arms open and imperfect eyesight.
Do not ask for your life's load lightened,
But for courage to endure.
Do not ask for fulfillment in all your life,
Do not ask for perfection in all you do,
But for the wisdom not to repeat mistakes.
And finally, do not ask for more,
Before saying, "Thank you,"
For what you have already received.
If you're looking for somebody to blame —
Look in the mirror.
There is no challenge that cannot be met,
And dream that cannot be achieved.

*Written by one of our
Covenant House kids*

Chapter 5

*"The last desperation stop at the
end of a long and painful road."*

September, 1993

I strained to make sense of the kids talking, but I
was way over my head. "Sounds like Chinese," our
intake leader Ed said. "But then again...."

"Look's like really bad news," I said.

There were six kids in all. Six terrified, shaking,
what-am-I-doing-here kids. The youngest was 14, the
oldest 17. I think they wanted to smile at me, but they
were too scared to do it.

"What's their story, Ed? Where'd these kids come
from?"

"Down from Chinatown, Sister. A police raid."

"A police raid?"

"Yuh, Sister, the cops broke into this brothel. The
vice squad brought in 22 illegal aliens in all, including
these kids. They were being held by an Asian gang.

"They have nowhere else to go, Sister. No where."
Ed leaned extra hard on the "nowhere," to make his
point. Big, tough, physically imposing, Ed's one of the
softest touches in the world when it comes to kids.
That's why he's so good at keeping a nightly vigil at
our front door.

"I know we are near full tonight, Sister, but...." I held up my hand before he could go on. "There's no such thing as 'no room,' Ed," I said. "I'll go grab the sleeping bags now," he said. He was smiling like a little kid....

"Andrew is coming over from the engine room and will be here in a minute, Sister. He speaks Chinese."

The oldest kid (five boys, one girl) jerked his eyes my way. I think the word "Chinese" got his attention....

The next three minutes were a blur. Andrew burst in and began talking to the kids in a language I didn't understand. The kids talked back all at once. The more Andrew talked, the more the kids relaxed. By the time he was finished, they were all smiling.

"Sister, these kids have been through hell the last 20 days. They are straight from China. They were kidnapped a few weeks ago, thrown onto a ship and sent over against their will. For the past week they've been held in a cheap hotel, and forced to have sex.

"And you know what else? They think this is a jail. That's why they're so scared. They think we're police."

"Tell them we're not," I said.

"I did," Andrew said. "I'm not sure they believe me yet."

"Take them down for some food," I said. "They look hungry," I said. Hungry for food, I thought. Hungry for caring that doesn't bruise or degrade, I thought.

Andrew spoke gently again to the kids. I nodded a

lot and pretended I knew what he was saying. They nodded a little and tried to smile, all of us speaking the same body language. They really were beautiful kids.

I checked up on them a few minutes ago in the cafeteria. They were all sitting at one table with Andrew, trying to make sense of their chicken, carrots and mashed potatoes. Our six newest kids looked very alone and very sad. Being 15,000 miles away from home, in a place you don't understand, will do that to a kid....

We're, of course, going to do everything we can for our six newest kids. Everything.

I mean, I know that "illegal aliens" (that term makes me cringe ... what could be illegal about being one of God's children?) aren't the most popular group in this country these days. No one's holding marches to protect them. We all know someone who would smirk at the idea of helping kids who "don't belong here in the first place."

All I know is, they are kids. Beautiful, scared, hungry, needy ... kids. This year, hundreds of these kids — 10, 14, 17, black, white, Hispanic, Asian — will come to Covenant House for the simple reason all our kids come to us. They have no other place to go. No options. Absolutely none.

Unable to speak, unsure who to trust, completely unaware how to survive, they end up on our laps. By crawling in or stumbling in. Many times, led by a policeman's hand. Covenant House isn't a "choice" for these kids. Kids like this don't get choices (it's hard to "give up" something you never had). We're quite simply the last desperation stop at the end of a long and indescribably painful road. Many of them, far, far more than we know, die before they even get this far.

What these kids have in common with our other kids is how good they are, and brave they are, and how passionately Jesus loves them. Maybe more than any other kids in the world, they have the right to be called the least of His Brethren. They will always have the right to be called a Covenant House kid.

I do know I find it impossible to turn these beautiful kids away. I just can't.

Please, maybe you could help them, and our 1,194 other super beautiful kids, too? (That's a lot of beautiful kids to love.)

Everything we are is because of you. All that we are able to accomplish in giving hope and love to six beautiful kids from China who can't possibly be illegal, and 1,194 other gorgeous kids, is because of you. You mean that much to these kids. (I guess that's just another way of saying you mean everything....)

P.S. I know that God has a very special place in His infinite heart for our six newest kids — I absolutely, positively know that. I'm sure — positively sure — He understands better than I ever could their deepening loneliness, their anxiety becoming fear becoming terror, their despair over the unknown fate that awaits them. The aloneness and fear and terror and abandonment all our kids feel ... they share that with Him in a very unique way.

Dear Sister Mary Rose,

I came to Covenant House after being in NY for about 8 months. I was admitted to the hospital the night before. I was beaten up by a crack dealer. When I walked through your doors I had hit a bottom that was indescribable. You gave me shelter, food, clothes, safety and hope. I still have the robe I wore that first night and also the rosary I made while I was there. Later, after living in a group home and re-hab my parents accepted me back into their home. Since then I have finished high school, and I work as a supervisor. I have also gotten married and bought a house. My life has made a 360 degree turn around and Covenant House was the start of making that happen.

L.S.

Run Away

Scared and cold,
first night on the streets
Your body hurts
from your head to your feet

You miss school,
not the work — it's the friends
Thinking what you'll say
when they ask
where you've been

Gota dollar-fifty,
every penny gota spend
Make a wrong move ... Boom -
your life comes to an end.

> Daniel, 16,
> a kid on the street

Chapter 6

*"I can't do this for my
mother, anymore."*

October, 1993

The 10-year-old boy came running into our crisis shelter this morning — frantic — scared out of his mind.

"I can't do it anymore," he said to Mattie at our front desk. "I just can't do this for my mother anymore."

At that moment, he reached into his pockets and placed 22 vials of crack and a gun on the shelf. The vials have a street value of $25 a piece. The gun was a 9 millimeter Uzi.

The little boy was crying.

"Please help me," he kept saying. "I just can't do this for my mother anymore...."

You're going to have a hard time believing this letter. What I need to tell you is almost too bizarre and implausible to believe.

It concerns something very new and very scary that we've seen happening out on the streets. *It's very, very important that you know about it....*

These last few months, our crisis team counselors have become increasingly alarmed about a new phenomenon running into our shelter — an exploding population of homeless *girls and boys who've been forced to run drugs for their parents*.

I'm sure you realize that there have always been scattered cases of this reprehensible activity before.

But now — this year, this month — the number of little kids forced to run drugs has begun to skyrocket! What had been a small trickle, has grown into a small stream — a stream of utterly defenseless, totally innocent kids like this 10-year-old boy who are over their heads and drowning on America's streets.

More and more, these little children are ending up on our doorstep because they've been asked to deal drugs by their parents ... and they're too terrified to do it anymore.

These parents use their children to run drugs because the kids are trustworthy, and innocent looking, and resourceful and yes, free of charge. But most of all, these kids are being used to run drugs, because they are the perfect "front man" for the crime ... and the best "insurance" that the deal will be completed.

"It's not likely that a drug dealer will shoot a 10-year-old boy, and steal the money," one policeman told me. "Kids that age just don't get shot at much. But it's not impossible either...."

These little kids are, in many ways, the poorest of the poor at Covenant House. They not only must somehow struggle to survive in a world without love and security. They must carry the incredible extra burden of breaking laws ... running drugs ... being insidiously used and wasted by parents who no longer care about them.

They come to us, for a very simple reason: they have no other place to go. There is no "Dickens-like," romantic aura surrounding them. They are hungry, and dirty, and many times dressed in tattered clothes. If you met them you'd be overwhelmed by how very, very terrified they are. And how very tiny and brave, too.

And they are still just little kids.

Please, please understand that these are not bad kids. It's very important you understand this. They are simply innocent kids placed in a situation — a nightmare, an unreal world — that has become the only world they know.

The little boy said it best, when Mattie asked him why he was carrying a 9 millimeter Uzi....

"I have to," he said.

"It comes with my job," he said.

"I sell drugs," he said.

What would you and I do if we were placed in his shoes? I mean, if I were 10 years old, and running "errands" for my mother was the only life I knew — the only life I knew! — would I know enough to escape? Could I? I really don't know the answer to that. I just don't....

I *do* know that we must do absolutely everything we can to care for this kid, and the hundreds of others like him. Now that God has brought him to us, we are going to do all we can to find this child a good home. A place where kids are loved and wanted and cared for.

A place every kid should know in his or her lifetime. I've made an absolute promise to him....

As for the others still out there, alone? We are doing all we can to rescue these kids, as many as we can. Thanks to dear friends like you, our van will be combing the city tonight, again searching in those dark, hidden corners that swallow up so many innocent children. And thanks to you, many of these innocent kids will be rescued. Many will find a new life, thanks to you....

But we need your help to continue this mission.

Please ... can you help us meet this very urgent need?

You must be awfully tired of getting these appeals to help our kids. I'm sure you have your own families to worry about, your own kids dear to your heart. But....

I've always felt that all of us who are connected to Covenant House — our volunteers, our workers, our very special donors like you — are truly the last, best hope for these kids. Every kid who will live tomorrow, every kid who will smile, every boy and girl who will feel loved this week for the first time ... will experience this hope because of you.

And why we help them — why wonderful people like you continue to save these kids — is one of the most beautiful things of all. Covenant House has never been about "guilt." We help these kids because there is something very good and beautiful inside all of us that tells us we *absolutely* must help them. A gut-level commitment which I believe was first inspired in each of us by God ... but has been nurtured by you.

It is that special covenant that makes this mission so very special. I really think the covenant you've made with these kids is one of the most beautiful things I've ever seen....

Dear Sister Mary Rose,

Your newsletter gives a reality-based perspective few child care experts have. Just over a decade ago I myself was a teen runaway, and your notes capture exactly how I felt at that time. I am now a proud mother of three with a Master's degree — your kids must never give up!

L.E.

My precious Jesus,
I am hurting. To write everything would fill this
book. You know my troubles, you know my ques-
tions and you know my answers. Please help me.
Give me strength and please give me what I need
to be happy. Please love and take care of my cats
and all the hungry people and creatures of the
world.

A prayer written
by a kid in our
Covenant House Chapel

Chapter 7

"Maybe it's because God
is carrying them on
His shoulders."

November, 1993

When me and the kids march to Times Square that night, *we will brush aside the pimps and pornographers that stand in our way*. I frankly don't care how angry they get at us....

For one shining night, we will gather under the glitz and glitter of Times Square and expose it for what it is. A concrete graveyard. Where thousands of kids have been buried inside neon tombstones with names like "ShowWorld."

I swear you'll be able to see God in every kid's face....

I'm about to make the pimps and pornographers really hate me again....

In fact, once they hear what I'm up to, some of the most vicious pimps in the world are going to want to strangle me.

You see, I've decided that the kids and I are going

to do it again — *we're going to again hold a special Candlelight Vigil for America's kids.*

And it's not going to be a "nice and quiet" vigil that no one knows about, and it's not going to be held where it's safe and we won't "bother" anyone.

I've decided that this year *every single Covenant House* in America is going to hold a Vigil smack-dab in the middle of the most dangerous places for children in America.

I've made a commitment to our kids that we're going to literally push aside the pimps and pornographers in rotten places like Times Square ... and spark a new flame of hope for America's forgotten kids.

Why another vigil? And what's going to make *this year's* special?

Well, I think the answer to that first question can be found on the faces — uncertain, scared — of every kid in America.

I don't have to tell you that this year — 1993 — has been an especially horrifying year for kids. It seems like every day, you and I have been bludgeoned with more and more grotesque headlines ... headlines about kids being beaten, forgotten, hurting, dying....

I can't stop thinking about these kids, and how much they desperately need you and me. *These children we read about are not nameless, faceless "characters" crammed beneath a sensational tabloid headline.*

They are real flesh and blood children. *Children who all too soon, are destined to be our next Covenant*

House kids.

30,000 of them will come to our doors this year. Many more will never find us.

And this comes at a time when every recent poll shows that the "issue of homelessness" is losing support among the American people. *While more kids are suffering on the street, fewer people care.*

(Thank God you do. We never stop thanking God for you.)

So we — people who care about our kids — are faced with a very clear choice right now.

We can wring our hands in despair, and hope that somehow, someway, things will get better for America's kids.

Or we can take a stand today — make our mark today — do all we can today — to fight back!!!!

That's why I'm holding this Candlelight Vigil again this year.

I don't have any naive, pie-in-the-sky illusions about our vigil. I know that you and I are not going to change the world overnight.

But I think — *I know from experience!* — that through our vigil we can begin to refocus it. To put a huge, don't-the-world-dare-think-this-problem-is-going-to-go-away microscope on a crushing national crisis that affects every one of our children.

And I know one other thing. *It's something that God has led me to do.* I feel an absolute conviction that He is reaching out to me today, and pushing me to take this step. It's something I absolutely positively *must* do. I can feel it with every ounce of my body.

If you've ever been to one of our Candlelight Vigils, you know why this vigil means so much to me....

It all starts around 5:00 as darkness falls, and something very magical begins to happen on the corners of 41st Street and 10th Avenue.

What will begin as a trickle of kids, and then grow to a steady stream, will wash onto the sidewalk outside our shelter. These kids — cold, hurting, sometimes bitter — are probably not the most beautiful kids in the whole world. But they are an inspiration and an example to me.

As this gaggle of kids swells to the tens, and then twenties and finally the hundreds, I will then have the honor of leading them in procession to the center of Times Square.

I think our kids all grow about four extra feet in stature during that walk. I know they feel something incredibly moving inside. Maybe it's knowing they are walking a path which has swallowed up so many kids who came before them. Maybe it's the sense of pride that's literally bursting out of their tired bodies. Maybe it's because God is carrying them on His shoulders....

(I'm not naive enough to forget that it might also be the presence of TV cameras which hover over our procession of candles, like moths flying to a flame. Thank God for them — last year's vigil was covered by all the major news outlets — we were able to spread the word and reach out to thousands of kids and families!!!)

Finally, the kids and I will stop at our final destination, the place where so many pimps and pornographers don't want us to be — the middle of Times Square. The world center of glitz and glitter. The national graveyard for America's lost and homeless kids.

For 60 shining minutes, though, Times Square will belong to you and me and our kids, and no one else.

For 60 minutes, our kids and our friends (in past years they've come as far as North Carolina, Arizona ... from all over) will stand together and reach out to God, for God. We'll say prayers together, and sing hymns together. We'll light candles of hope and prayer. Our kids will speak up and speak out, bringing traffic to a standstill. The media, often so cynical, will see and feel the beauty of our kids.

And each of us at the moment — the believing and the disbelieving, the kids praying up to the sky and the pimps staring at the sidewalk aching for us to just go away — we'll all feel God among us and truly inside us.

Please watch over these kids of ours, God, we'll say. To those kids new to the street and who still have a chance, help them find us. To those kids sinking in the quicksand of the street and frantically reaching out for a lifeline, help them discover us. To those who are walking out their final days of a nightmarish teenage death sentence, help us shower them with our love until they get to heaven and You engulf them with Yours.

Our prayers will be answered quickly. During the vigil, lots of kids will see our candles, which hang over Times Square like that star hung over Bethlehem that night. And they will come.

And even after we finish our final prayer, and begin our long procession through Times Square back to the shelter, the light won't go away. God will see to that. No one can extinguish the flame we'll leave living and breathing under neon lights.

Now, can you see why I believe so passionately in this vigil? Why I'd rather be in Times Square on that night than any other place in the world?

I believe with all my heart that there is only one question facing us in the service of our lost generation of kids — what would Jesus do? I know the answer cannot be found in merely "worrying" about our kids — but in walking straight into the lion's den to let them know we are still here. (To not only love our kids, but to be their servants.)

Can you be there with me? I'd love to stand with you during our vigil in Times Square. As I mentioned, some have come thousands of miles to be with us at our previous vigils. Please consider coming, if you can....

And even if you can't make it, please let me know you'll be there with us in spirit. Your prayers will mean a lot to me and the kids who'll be there in Times Square that night. Please.

I believe this Candlelight Vigil is a pure, demonstrable expression of everything that is good and

decent and right about Covenant House and our kids.
And that your prayers with us can and will make a difference. Please, please continue to pray for our kids
and help them if you can....

Dear Sister Mary Rose,

*God bless you for holding that vigil for the kids! I
lit a candle at 5:45 and was saying the prayer you sent
and then I saw you and your children in Times Square
on CBS news with Dan Rather — it looked so cold. I
prayed doubly hard that God will bless your cause and
all your kids worldwide.*

*P.S. Please be extra careful again at next year's vigil. I
was concerned about the possibility that some of
the children who were brought into "slavery" by
pimps and pornographers might grab one of the
kids. It would not be right if even one of the children were identified to be recaptured or injured in
any way.*

G.N.

Help Me

Help me, Dear Lord
    as I travel towards You.
There are many detours
    which will try to distract
    me away from You.
Help me as I travel my path
    to cherish the parents You gave me.
Help me to do my best in all my endeavors
    whether I may win or lose.
Help me never to lose hope
    though there may be difficult times.
Help me to choose good friends.
Help me to choose the right mate,
    so that I may have a happy family someday.
Help me, though I may fall,
    to continue on my journey towards You.
Help me, Dear Lord.
I want so much to be with You. Amen.

                Written by a
                Covenant House kid

Chapter 8

*"I wish you could be here then ...
to see the miracle."*

Christmas, 1993

Someday Christmas is going to be easy again.

Someday, when I'm too old for this job, I'll be sitting at my dining room table on Christmas Eve, surrounded by my Sisters.

And on that Christmas, we'll be doing what we always used to do — we'll be thinking about the Baby of Bethlehem and eating good food, and singing Christmas carols, and laughing, and loving each other.

Christmas will be a lot easier then.

Christmas here at Covenant House is *not* easy.

There is a miracle that occurs here every Christmas, and witnessing it is more meaningful than any happy Christmas I ever spent ... but it is definitely *not* easy.

I know what will happen here on Christmas Eve.

On December 24th, around 5:00 PM, a 15-year-old girl named Erica will stumble in the door bruised and bloodied because her pimp beat her up. Even though Erica is just a girl, and it's Christmas Eve, the pimps won't care. They never do....

On Christmas Eve, a young boy named Steve will

crack, and come to us in tears. Steve will go over the edge because of all the happiness he sees on the faces of the people he passes in front of department store windows. "I never had anything like that, Sister," he'll say. "I never had a nice Christmas...."

We'll spend half the night easing Steve's pain.

On Christmas Eve, hundreds more kids — dirty, hungry, frozen and infinitely sad — will wander into Covenant House. There is no mystery why they will be led to us. These desperate kids will come for the same reason kids have come for every other Christmas Eve — they have nowhere else to go that night. No place to call home. Nothing to call their own.

Of course, when I see these kids on our doorstep that night, I'll see God in every one of their faces.

I mean, it's very, very easy to see Jesus in the tired, dirty faces of street kids like Erica and Steve, standing in the cold twilight in torn sneakers, wrapped in dirty clothes.

I mean, the life Jesus lived was not unlike the life my kids lead today. The young-adult Jesus we see in today's Christmas cards — a Jesus in flowing robes, clean, inwardly content and outwardly revered — that simply wasn't the reality Jesus lived back then.

Jesus was in many ways an outcast, a wanderer, an often lonely figure alternately condemned and ridiculed by the power brokers of His time.

His struggle to gain acceptance, much less save us, was all-consuming and always, a battle that began right at birth.

The Holy Men of His day loudly and openly questioned what good could possibly come out of Bethlehem. Bethlehem was a dark, lonely place. Certainly not a place of power. How could someone all-powerful come from "there," they asked? Someone who'll lead us, born in Bethlehem?

When you stop to think of Jesus in this way — a baby born into a world of darkness and doubt, a teenager living in a world of rejection and pain — it's not hard to see Him in the faces of our kids.

In fact, I think the Christmas story belongs to our kids in a way it belongs to no one else. Many of our kids have been born into a cold, cruel world, with a lot of people who aren't willing to accept them, or give them the love and hope they need.

And like the Christ Child before them, our kids desperately need someone to watch over them and love them. To believe in them, like the Wise Men believed 1,993 years ago....

Thanks to you, these kids will know that special love this Christmas.

This Christmas Eve, we'll shower these kids with good food, and clean clothes, and smother them with a parent's love (knowing all the while we can never, ever be as good as the real thing). We'll stand hand in hand with them after our Midnight Mass, and we'll sing carols together. We'll hug each other a hundred times, and tell stories to each other, and share that magical Christmas Eve love with each other.

And after our Mass, each kid at Covenant House

will go to sleep feeling — truly feeling down deep in their souls — a tranquility they may have never felt before on Christmas Eve.

In the dark and stillness, a miracle will happen — a Christmas miracle.

The star will rise over Bethlehem. The angels will sing softly. The shepherds will say "Peace on Earth."

And in the morning the Christ Child will be born again ... in the faces of our kids.

Their problems won't have disappeared. The miracle of Christmas doesn't work like that. But there will be something different, even if only for one day....

Erica's bruises will still be purple, but they will be softened by a new light in her eyes. Steve will still have the same life he hates, but his step will be lightened by the glimmer of hope in his heart.

Every kid without a home will stand near our Christmas tree and be surrounded by a truly loving family. And somehow, the Christmas carols will sound like hymns of joy such as you've never heard before.

I wish you could be here then ... to see the miracle. To see God in each of their faces....

You would truly see the real spirit of Christmas then. Not a "Ho, Ho, Ho," kind of spirit, but the real unbridled joy of a cold, dark world being lit by the Star of Bethlehem.

Yes, Christmas is not easy here. *Yet, Christmas here is the best way I have actually experienced God's gift to the world.*

Of course, all of it is possible because of you. The

Christmas miracle of Covenant House simply wouldn't happen without you. That's why my first prayer on Christmas morning is always one of thanks that you found us. Always....

God bless you. And may you and those you love enjoy a most blessed Christmas. Our kids and I will be praying for you.

Dear Sister Mary Rose,

I can't get your Christmas letter out of my mind. I used to be a street kid many years ago, and I know all too well about the loneliness your kids feel that day.

The holidays make you feel even lonelier when everyone else is home with family. But you get used to it because you try not to let anyone else feel sorry for you so you just smile as if it's no big deal. Sometimes you even make up stories and say you have plans when someone invites you over so I know everything those kids are feeling....

T.G.

Dear Lord,
Thank you for taking care of me. I never had no
one to care about me. Oh and I'm sorry for what
happened yesterday. Lord, you know why I want
to stay here, because I don't trust anybody on the
streets right now. Danger is always going on. I
wish I could get adopted by a nice person. I've
never been treated nice or like a daughter. Lord
I send wishes for my family and friends.

A prayer written
by a kid in our
Covenant House Chapel

Chapter 9

"I got no place to go."

January, 1994

"No thanks, Sister," the tiny voice called out from the shadows. "I'll be OK. Don't worry."

The tiny kid standing in the darkness felt his voice crack, and I knew he was lying.

I caught the lump in my throat, and tried to stay cool.

For several nights, our Covenant House van team had pursued the 10-year-old boy, pulling alongside him to offer help, but never acting so anxious or scared for him that he would pull away.

"Do you need a place to stay — can we help you — will you come with us?" we asked him every night.

"No, I'll be all right," the tiny voice said, trying to act like he meant it.

I could see the longing in his eyes every time he said no. I kept praying to God that he'd change his mind, before it was too late. I knew time was running out for him....

Finally, tonight, the big breakthrough came.

Tonight, when he stepped out of the shadows, his face was black and blue and swollen and dripping tears that he had hidden from us before.

"I'm scared," he finally said. "I got no place to go."

I reached out and hugged him as hard as I could, but he was shaking so hard I couldn't get a good grip. Before I could jump out of the van, he was already on the pavement, sobbing.

He was still crying when we finally got him into a bed at our crisis center.

We don't even know his name. He's been too tired and embarrassed and proud to give it to us.

I can't get him out of my mind this morning. I wonder what he's thinking now, if he's dreaming. I wonder if he's *ever* for even one day lived a life that you or I would want to live? Even for one day....

I already imagine what he'll say to me the first time we talk.

"Hi, my name is ____," he'll say. "I'm sorry I put you through all this trouble," he'll say. "This is really embarrassing ending up like this." (You'd be amazed how many of our kids are overwhelmed with embarrassment when they come to our shelter. For all their hurt, and pain and incredible sorrow, street kids are most scared of being looked down on. Of smelling bad, and looking dirty. As if being 15 and homeless and unwanted is all their fault....)

"I ... I don't have any place to go, Sister," the boy will then tell me. "I wish I did, but my (fill in the blank ... stepmother, father, parents ...) beat me, and I couldn't live there anymore.

"No one loves me," the boy will say.

"I tried to survive on the streets, Sister, I really did.

But I was too tired and too hungry...."

And then, in the quiet of tonight, this little kid who is still so tired he can barely keep his eyes open, and so hurt and lonely he can't remember the last time anyone hugged him (if anyone has *ever* hugged him), will break down again and cry.

I will let him know that we truly care for him, and that he can stay with us as long as he likes, and that yes, we truly do love him.

And, like every Covenant House kid, he will look at me with tear-filled eyes, half disbelieving and half wondering, and he'll say, "Thanks, Sister. Thanks for taking me in."

And I will thank God at that moment for you.

Dear Sister Mary Rose,

Ten years ago our son, then 15, ran away to New York to find excitement. His big adventure ended at Covenant House where he spent two nights before coming home again. The experience made a deep impression on him and it made us all realize the value of Covenant House, especially for kids who have no place to go home to!

P.C.

Dear Father,

I just want to ask for your help in the time I'm away from my mother and please help me in my actions and my attitude towards people because I know it has got real bad. And Lord please help me in the rest of my teen years because the last five years of my life have been the worst.

I am here Lord to rededicate my life and to comfort my family. I thank you for my life and for the staff members, counselors and Pastors at Covenant House. I need a Bible.

A prayer written
by a kid in our
Covenant House Chapel

Chapter 10

"I love you, Mom."

February, 1994

"I'm bad news, Sister," the skeleton said.

"I've been around and seen it all," he said.

"Believe me ... there ain't nobody who wants me."

The boy leaned hard on the word "nobody" and shifted in his seat. I could tell he was dying for me to tell him he was wrong. He was a beaten kid. Sad. Weathered. And very, very ill.

His skinny frame heaved and rattled every time he coughed.

The skeleton was eighteen....

"I want to be your friend," I said. "Will you let me?" He looked down and hacked out a yes. "What's your name?" I said.

"Joey," he coughed. "From California."

"That's a long way away," I said. "Yes," he said. "Do you want to tell me what happened," I said.

"It's not easy," he said. He looked like he was about to start crying. "Please try," I said.

He cleared his throat and plunged in. I could tell this was going to hurt a lot. "I ... I used to have a home," he said. "But then ... then my dad died," he said. His eyes began to brim over.

"Me and my mom ... we started to have trouble. She was always stressed out ... yelling ... screaming. I guess she couldn't take it. It wasn't just her fault, Sister ... it was mine, too. I couldn't take it either...."

"I started doing bad stuff ... stuff like drugs. And then a new guy moved into the house ... he started beating me. I just couldn't take it anymore. So I just ran. I had to get out, you know what I mean?"

"Where'd you run to," I said.

"Nowhere," he said. "And everywhere. I mean, I hitched up with another guy and we just jumped on a boxcar, and headed east. It was kind of exciting at first, seeing new places, meeting new people. But then my money ran out. The last 10 months have been like living in hell," he said. "It's been really hard just getting through the day." His voice trailed off, and the tears began to stream down his face.

"What about your mom," I said. "Moms can be really forgiving. Do you ever think about calling her," I said.

He looked over at me for the longest time, stood up, and then dug deep into his back pocket. Slowly, and ever so cautiously, he pulled a yellowed, tattered photograph out and placed it on my desk.

It was a picture of Joey with his mother. "I think about her all the time," he said. "But I'm too scared to call her now. I bet she hates me now, after what I did...."

"Tell me her number," I said, reaching for the telephone. "Let's ask her," I said.

Joey's mouth and eyes sprang open as he gave me the phone number. He grimaced and fidgeted while I dialed.

Seconds later a woman, crazy with joy, began shouting and weeping at the other end of the phone.

"My son ... Joey ... my son," she cried. "Please let me speak to him."

By the time I handed Joey the phone he was crying. "Hi mom ... it's me ... do you forgive me ... I miss you so much mom. I'm sorry."

"I love you, mom," he kept crying.

For the next half hour Joey and his mom cried and talked and cried on the phone. Last night, while most of us slept, Joey got on an overnight airplane and headed home — to the only home he ever knew — to see a mother he thought he would never see again.

It was beautiful seeing him get on that plane. As he walked through the gate, I just stood there, enjoying this beautiful victory. And when I saw his plane take off, I realized Joey was a special gift to us from God ... a very beautiful Lenten gift.

"I wish they were all this easy, God" I said to Him. "I wish they were all this easy....

I really don't like Lent. It's not something we're supposed to like, I guess.

I mean, Lent is all about tough questions. It's all about things we must ask ourselves, and reckoning, and looking in the mirror and seeing if we like what's staring back at us.

It's a time to reflect on how we use the goods of

the world, and how we deal with our relationships. It's a time to think back if we're really trying to live a life of love, a time to look under the hood of our souls to make sure everything's running all right and see where the defects are. It's a time to make resolutions to turn our lives around, and then begin the painful process of dealing with those resolutions....

It's not easy spending forty days staring into the mirrors of our souls, scrutinizing, writing checklists, grading performance. It's not easy asking ourselves if we're really being as good as we want to be, as virtuous, as steadfast, as understanding. But it's good for us I think. Lent is that one time when we are most in touch with God.

Our kids? Kids like Joey? I think they experience Lent better than many of us ever will. Our kids live in a perpetual Lent ... a nonstop life of painful reckoning, questioning, excruciating self-examination, of losses.

I mean, you and I may "give up things" these next forty days by choice. Our kids have spent an entire lifetime "giving up things" ... things that no kid should ever be forced to give up.

They "give up" home because they've been battered and abused so much they simply can't live there anymore. In running to the street or hopping on a box-car, they "give up" all hope of being loved. They "give up" all hope of being cared for. Of feeling secure. Of being loved.

Lent is in their hearts every minute of their lives.

It makes it all the more beautiful when you can see

the resurrection happening in their lives.

Thank you so much for reading this letter, and praying for our kids. You mean the world to us, you really do. And we never, ever stop thanking God you found us. Never! Especially during Lent....

Dear Sister Mary Rose,

I remember about 5 months ago when I was thrown out of my home because my father was "sick of hearing me," I was glad I could call your NINELINE (1-800-999-9999) for help. Being without a mom because she died and having a father who hated me and wished I'd leave, I was so glad you were there for me. It's ironic how I call you for help and yet I help the kids who need it. Thanks for everything!

J.S.

Our Love

Sometimes I wonder how people
  judge our love,
They never seem to notice that it
  comes from Heaven above.
But if our love is strong and true
  and solid to the soul,
Then listening to them is not
  what we'll do.
Our love will be bold.
The love we have will shine
  through storms,
No matter how rough the times.
Forever and ever, we'll be
  together like the sun.
Yes, it will shine.

Written by a
Covenant House kid

Chapter 11

"I guess I'm a real reject, huh?"

March, 1994

I had to bury a kid today.

I'm really having trouble dealing with the pain.

Her name was Brenda, and I loved her a lot. I mean, I love all our kids, but Brenda was something very, very special, a very wonderful gift handed to all of us by God.

Brenda was 16 years old.

She came to our California center three weeks ago, out of the blue, a scared little waif in dirty blue jeans and stringy hair, running away from the life she knew in a desperate attempt to find a life she wanted. Brenda was running to escape her gang. I was in California that day to see all the kids.

I'm sure God arranged the whole meeting....

"Will this 'shelter place' (her words) let me sleep here tonight?" she asked.

"I don't want to be in a gang, anymore," she said. "I can't live like this anymore," she said. "Please ... can I stay here?"

"Of course," we said. "We love you," we said. "Does that mean yes?" she said. "That means yes," we said.

She carried inside a little knapsack and a frantic set of eyes that never seemed to close, never seemed to stop scanning whichever room she entered.

Believe me, it's unusual and scary for a gang kid like Brenda to come to Covenant House, or anywhere else. Kids — *especially* rejected, hurting, alone kids — feel a certain comfort in being in a gang, being "part of something." It's comforting to see the same faces every day. It's nice feeling accepted, like a peer. It's great not feeling like you're being judged every moment.

Gangs quickly become substitute families for kids like Brenda. In Brenda's case, it was the only family she had....

"I don't have a home, Sister," she had told me when I met her. "I wish I had a home to live in, but I don't. I wish I had a mother who could take care of me, but I don't. *She's not bad,* Sister. She just can't handle life anymore.

"Last year, she just told me and my brother to leave. 'I can't care for you anymore,' she said. 'I'm sorry, but I can't.' So, I left....

"But I couldn't take being in a gang, so I left that, too. I guess I'm a real reject, huh?" she said.

"Of course you're not," I said.

It was beautiful watching Brenda grow these last few weeks (even if I had to do my "watching" 3,000 miles away.) I think our love knocked her over like a ton of bricks. I mean, we (you and me) kind of overwhelmed her! I don't think she ever dreamed she'd be loved like we loved her!

Her dirty, tired skin began to glow. Her walk quickened and lightened. Her eyes stopped darting across every room she entered, and she learned to relax.

We really had big plans for Brenda. She was going to be one of those extra special kids who didn't just "make" it, but flourished. I know with a little love and help, she could have done anything. Anything.

But then it began to fall apart.

"I'm going out to see some friends," she told one of our counselors. "I'm only gonna be an hour or so."

"I'm not leaving Covenant House," she said. "I don't want to stay out there," she said. "I just want to take a walk. I'll only be gone an hour or so. Promise!"

After more than an hour had passed, the California staff grew worried. Lonny, our night supervisor, couldn't take the waiting anymore, and went searching for Brenda, running block after block, in the middle of the night, calling out her name.

Brenda never called back. She couldn't.

That night, while standing on the street corner talking to a friend, Brenda was shot in the heart. The bullet was aimed for someone else, but it struck her.

Brenda was killed instantly.

The funeral was this morning, and like most funerals it was painful, and wrenching, and awful, and uplifting and hard. I had trouble even looking into the coffin. I kept wanting to cry.

A lot of Brenda's old gang members — some tough, crusty, seen-it-all-kids — were crying like babies, too. It was impossible not to cry....

The homily was beautiful. Father Matt spoke from his heart, and spoke directly to the gang members a lot. He talked a lot about God's infinite love, and compassion, and mercy. His words filled the church, echoing in the vaulted space above our heads:

Jesus said to the crowd: "All that the Father gives me shall come to me; no one who comes to me will I ever reject."

It was John's gospel, Chapter 6. And Father Matt repeated that line at least half a dozen times. He directed his talk to the kids grouped in the pews to his right, for the most part ignoring our staff and the other adults gathered in this place. You may think you're bad, he told the kids, you may think you are beyond redemption; but Jesus says,

"No one who comes to me will I ever reject."

"He has not rejected Brenda. He will not reject you."

I'm really having trouble writing this. I keep tearing up. I can't say why Brenda had to suffer as she did in her brief life, and why she had to die. I can only tell you that we'll love the next kid who knocks on our door as deeply and profoundly as we love Brenda. And the next and the next and the next....

"No one who comes to me will I ever reject."

I know it sounds strange, but I think Brenda lived a lifetime in the three weeks she was with us. I believe she came to know, and accept, in that short time what Father Matt was trying to tell the kids gathered at her funeral.

That we will not reject you.

That we will not turn you away.

That we will, in fact, love you.

Because we want to.

And, because we believe we are called to act in Jesus' place.

Covenant House has the privilege of being the instrument of our charity and generosity for troubled kids. In your name, we kept our part of God's promise of unconditional love to Brenda. With your help, we will always keep that promise....

P.S. I hope this letter doesn't get you down. You should be so very, very proud of what you do for our kids, even if we sometimes can't save them all. I mean, last year three out of every 10 kids we rescued off the streets we rescued for good ... not just for a night or a week but for the rest of their lives. *No one else is as successful in saving these kids as we are.* No one. Please remember that when you kneel down to say your prayers tonight. You really do work miracles for our kids. We never stop thanking God for you....

Dear Sister Mary Rose,

I read your letter about Brenda, and I am praying for her soul!

I spent a week at Covenant House in Florida four

years ago. I was pregnant and alone. The counselors at Covenant House were extraordinarily compassionate, unconditionally loving people. The week I spent there was the most enlightening experience of my life.... I have a healthy little girl, a full-time job, and am attending college. I truly believe that my time at "the Cov" strongly influenced my life decisions from then on and led me to where I am now.

J.H.

Dear Heavenly Father,

Please give me the strength to go on through my stay at Covenant House. Give me the wisdom and the knowledge to do what is right and not wrong. And please give me the strength to make the right decisions about the things that occur. I know I haven't been making the right decisions, but I'd like to better that. Life has not been easy for me through these times, but I know that you will give me the strength to go on for I do believe in you and all you say and do. Amen.

A prayer written
by a kid in our
Covenant House Chapel

Chapter 12

"It's not hard to believe in a resurrection, when you see it every day."

Easter, 1994

It's pretty fashionable being a cynic nowadays.

I mean, cynicism has become one of the really burgeoning growth industries in America, right up there with microchips and tabloid talk shows. I'm actually having trouble remembering the last day that passed when I didn't hear a TV show, newsperson, political leader or self-professed expert tell me how wrong, out-of-date, or just plain stupid some of my beliefs are.

It's getting to the point where you and I are supposed to feel guilty believing in "old things" like good manners, straight talk, chastity, monogamy, hard work, fair discipline, loyalty and playing life by the rules.

Imagine ... we've been wrong all these years!

I've really been getting kind of fed up with this lately. I mean, I find myself thinking about it a lot these days, especially now that it's almost Easter.

You know, *I really do wonder what would happen* if The Resurrection happened today.

I can see the questions now....

"How did you pull off that dead trick," the cynics would ask. "Who helped you do it? Where's your proof it actually happened? And who is this Mary you talk about? Do you really expect us to believe that she's a virgin? Have you got a good lawyer? Can I give you someone's name?"

OR MAYBE ... or maybe something even worse would happen. Maybe we've gotten so cynical, most people wouldn't even care....

I really wonder ... would a society that's been weaned on Oprah and Phil and Geraldo, reality shows and shock TV, even sit up and take notice, much less believe? Would it be considered 'significant'? Would a risen Jesus Christ be given more time on Phil or Geraldo than the most recent tantalizing topic? Would any of them give Him 60 minutes on prime time?

I know one thing. It wouldn't be easy for believers like you and me. All of us who said we believed in this resurrection ... it wouldn't be easy for us.

I mean, would people nowadays accept the fact that we believe in this resurrection, simply because ... well, we *believe.*

Is a pronouncement that *we have faith* enough nowadays to satisfy those who don't? Would people let us enjoy our basic belief, that faith, which can't really be logically explained but is in each of us, because ... well, *it is?*

Would simply saying *"I believe"* be explanation enough for the skeptics, when all logic and reason tells us that a resurrection simply isn't possible?

I think it would be really tough for us believers in 1994. Really tough....

I guess that's because believing isn't easy. It's far easier to take a position of skepticism than to put yourself on the line.

And when the question is your faith in God? That's when it really gets tough. It's not always easy talking about Jesus and His resurrection, much less explaining it. This *ability to believe* is itself a gift from God. We can be grateful for this gift even if we don't understand it.

Our kids? What do they believe? A resurrection simply isn't something a street kid thinks about, much less understands.

I mean, it's tough for a homeless kid who's been dying on the street to understand the passionate love of the Father or the mystery of His salvation and redemption. For most of our kids, the harsh reality of their lives doesn't leave much room for wondering about a Jesus who loved them so much, He died for them 2,000 years ago. Our kids are consumed with more temporal questions — like "what's going to happen to me," ... "why doesn't anyone want me," ... "where will I sleep tonight...."

Maybe it's enough for these kids that you and I pray for them. And love them. And care for them. Even if they don't understand when we talk about Jesus and His resurrection.

So this Easter I'll keep praying for our kids, and thanking God for them. All the kids, lost and lonely and hurting. And I'll say an extra big prayer of thanks for the kids who give us the most hope, the kids who *are* being reborn here, the ones slowly but surely beginning a personal resurrection of their own.

Maybe that's the best lesson you and I will learn from Covenant House. That we *are* an Easter people. We *are* about resurrection and light. And we have the honor of carrying that light into the lives of our kids. It's not hard to believe in a resurrection in 1994 when you see it every day. I know I'm blessed to see so many Easters in my life....

Thanks for making it all possible. GOD BLESS YOU! And may you and all those you love enjoy a most blessed Easter. You can be sure we'll all be praying for you....

Dear Sister Mary Rose,

Our 3rd daughter has been rebellious at times and has caused us a great deal of worry. When she began reading the letters at age 13, it gave me a perfect opportunity to show how God works with us in our lives. Without a doubt, the letters about teenagers in trouble gave our daughter a real challenge to think about her family, and God, and life. I'm very thankful that we had the letters to talk about.

G.H.

"On the street I saw a girl cold and shivering in a thin dress, with little hope of a decent meal. I became angry and said to God: "Why did you permit this? Why don't you do something about it?" For a while God said nothing. That night He replied quite suddenly: "I certainly did something about it. I made you."

Chapter 13

*"He told me there was only
one thing in the world I
knew how to do."*

May, 1994

She sauntered over to the van, hips swaying in her short white shorts, acting cooler than cool.

But her eyes betrayed her. There was nothing happy inside them.

"Can't get too excited about nothin' when you're out on the street, man," she said.

"It's really good to see you, Bernetta," we said.

We all felt like just throwing our arms around her that first night, but we couldn't. Bernetta was like a skittish colt, and the last thing we wanted to do was scare her off. We were determined to take things slow.

So was she. At first, all she would accept was a cup of lemonade. Then she'd head back to 25th and 9th, the corner of New York City her pimp owned ... all pimps have their "territory"... and hustle for the rest of the night.

But after a few visits, Bernetta began to stay a little longer. Sometimes, she'd accept a cheese sandwich. And slowly, she began to reveal a little more of herself.

In fact, getting to know Bernetta was like peeling

layers off an onion. Including the tears.

"I was already 'broken in' before I got to the city," she said one night, shrugging her shoulders. "My step-dad, he raped me the first time when I was nine.

"Then, whenever he had a little to drink, he'd come creeping into my bedroom, late at night.

"One night, I tried putting a chair up against the door to keep him out. It worked pretty good. But the next day, he was so mad, he smashed that chair to bits, and gave me a black eye.

"He told me if I ever said a word, he'd hurt me bad. Course, he already had...."

Her voice trailed off and she looked inside our van, blinking furiously to drive back the teardrops that hung precariously in the corner of each eye.

She shook her head and swallowed hard.

"After a few years, I left. But I couldn't do nothin', I never finished school. I couldn't get a job.

"Then I met Freddie (her pimp). He told me there was only one thing in the world I knew how to do, and if I wanted to stay alive on the streets, I better do what I know best.

"I guess he was right," she said, smiling ruefully.

"He's not right, and don't you believe it," we said furiously. We could tell Bernetta was startled. That's why we usually try not to let kids see our anger.

But sometimes we can't help it.

These young girls come from across America to New York City, looking to escape from men ... fathers, brothers, friends, men they loved and trusted ... who have stolen their innocence and shattered their dreams.

By the time they get onto the streets, their self-esteem could fit onto the head of a pin.

Then their pimp tells them that they're good for nothing, that they deserve nothing — and that tiny speck of self worth disappears. Or turns into self loathing. Or gets buried in some deep, secret place.

"Bernetta, we want you to come back to Covenant House with us." Her eyes clouded over with fear.

"I can't. Freddie would kill me. He doesn't even know I talk to you guys. I can't, I just can't."

She began to sob.

"You know where Covenant House is?" we asked. She nodded. "You have one of our cards?" She nodded again.

We touched her hand. "We're going to say an extra prayer for you." (We didn't know then just how much she would need that prayer.)

She smiled through the tears and headed back to her corner of hell.

A few nights ago, the van swung by the corner of 25th and 9th, as we always do. We were really hoping to see Bernetta.

But when we got to the corner and started to pull up to the curb, Bernetta frantically waved us back.

Then she turned on her heel and started walking in the opposite direction.

We pulled away and headed down the street. But we were uncomfortable. And not a little scared. Something was very, very wrong.

So we turned the corner and headed back up the block. When we got there, I saw why Bernetta had tried to warn us off.

Her pimp held her against the wall with one arm. With the other, he punched and slapped her across the face and screamed obscenities.

"Who do you think you're talking to in that van, girl? You want to talk, you talk to me!"

When he spotted the van, he grabbed Bernetta by the hair and dragged her out of sight.

We drove after Bernetta and her pimp, but they escaped down a narrow alleyway.

A few hours later we came back to find her. She was back on the corner. But when we tried to come near, she shook her head and waved us away.

That was a few nights ago.

I think about Bernetta all the time. I think about her sad, empty eyes, and hope that there's still a twinkle hidden deep inside. Mostly, I hope she hung on to that card.

And I pray that God will show her the way to our door.

What I would like to ask this month is that you add your prayers to mine. Pray that Bernetta looks deep into her heart and finds that little speck of self-esteem that I know is buried there.

Pray that she has the strength to take the biggest step of her life ... away from her pimp, away from the street, and onto the steps of the only place in New York City where she can be safe — Covenant House.

I described Bernetta to all our staff members, and asked them to let me know when she arrives, whether it's 6 o'clock in the morning or midnight.

Because I want to be there at the door to greet her, and tell her how glad I am she came.

My friend, I hope she does make it to our door. With your prayers, and a little help from Him, I think she will.

Dear Sister Mary Rose,

I was one of those kids on the street. I was addicted to drugs and alcohol and my family missed all the warning signs. With no help from anyone, GOD was with me. I have almost two years been clean and sober. My recovery has helped me to go on to College to obtain my (CAC) Certified Alcoholism Counselor. I am 25 years old and Sister Mary Rose I have never felt so lucky to be alive. I thank GOD daily.

J.G.

Dear Lord,

I believe in you but I am so confused about where I'm going — all I know is where I've been. I am so scared and I have no one to talk to but myself and I hide my feelings in my music.

> *A prayer written*
> *by a kid in our*
> *Covenant House Chapel*

Chapter 14

*"She said she wasn't making
any money on me."*

June, 1994

He walked right up to me, and launched into it
without any preambles. He was 16 years old, and he
was a little desperate and very tired, so he decided to
get right to the point.

"Sister, how much do you get paid to take care of
me?" he asked.

*"I mean, how much does the state give you? Do
they give you a lot?"*

I could tell by Ricky's face there was something in
this question much deeper than a curiosity about the
finances of Covenant House. It isn't often a 16 year old
gets curious about who pays for the food and rent.

"Why do you want to know, Ricky?"

"Well, it's just ... I was just wondering."

"Are you worried about something?"

"Well, I figured that if you were getting paid by the
state to take care of me, then you'd probably keep me
around.

"I mean, you'd *have* to keep me around to get the
money, right?" He bit off the word "have" for extra
emphasis.

How on earth do these kids become so jaded so fast?

When Ricky walked in here yesterday, we didn't ask him a lot of questions about his past. We wanted to make sure he felt welcome. He told us he was 16 and that he had been on the street for *six months* ... ever since his mother threw him out of the house.

He was so exhausted when he walked in that he could barely keep his eyes open. He said he had a hard time sleeping on the street because he was scared all the time. He said there were very scary people on the streets.

He just woke up from his safe bed at Covenant House a little while ago, *after sleeping for 24 hours.*

"Ricky, money has nothing to do with it. I would want you here if I didn't have a penny in the world. We love you. Now, why did you ask that question?"

"Well ... that's what my mother said when she threw me out. She said she got money from the state for the foster children she took in and if I was gone she could take one more foster child.

"So she told me to get out. *She said she wasn't making any money on me.* I'm her son! She said those other kids were worth more than me. She told ME to get out, Sister!"

Ricky looked up at me, lost in his words. Tears rolled down his face. "Can you believe that, Sister," he kept saying. "Can you believe that?"

I reached out for him, and hugged him for a minute. I could believe it.... Tragically, I hear stories like this all too often. But it doesn't make Ricky's story any easier to accept....

Answers? Solutions? I don't have any.

I wish I did, but I don't. Because of the spiraling breakdown of the American family, more and more kids are freefalling alone, without the safety net of a place to call home. Because of massive budget cuts, programs to help these kids are becoming increasingly invisible (when budgets get cut, children's programs are traditionally cut to bits. Kids don't march, they don't vote, they don't send money to political campaigns).

And while the need grows and the "means" shrink, an incredibly dedicated, well-meaning but shrinking army of overworked, under-appreciated social workers are doing their best to find a place for these kids.

Somehow, amidst all the good intentions, kids become little living and breathing commodities. Some slip through the cracks. Some, like Ricky, are literally pushed out their front door, and told to make it on their own. It's terrible, it's wrong, and it hurts.

And once again, Covenant House stands as the last stop at the end of the dead-end street, ready to pick up the pieces.

I really didn't know how to answer Ricky's question. So I gave him the only answer I could.

"Ricky, we'll always be here for you, no matter what. There is no one more valuable than you in the entire world. You are priceless. I know that, and I'll never forget it. You don't have to worry now."

I think I caught him a little by surprise. "Thanks, Sister," he said. "You mean it?" he said. "That's really nice," he said.

"Our pleasure," I said. I saw Ricky again about an hour ago, and he ducked around a corner. I think he's still afraid we might change our mind and tell him it's time to leave.

I'll make sure I give him more reassurance tomorrow. Until then, thanks for praying for him, if you can. We never, ever stop thanking God you found us.

Dear Sister Mary Rose,

I finally read your letter and when I read about Ricky I had to cry. You see, we lost our son in March not from drugs or alcohol but from a doctor's negligence.... Since his death it has been very difficult holding on to my faith. I've often thought how unfair it was that such a special child had to die. Thank you Sister for sending this letter. It has reminded me that all God's children are equal in His eyes and should be in mine.

T.M.

*"I bound myself by oath,
I made a covenant with you ...
and you became mine."*

Ezekiel 16:8

*(Our oath, the first thing kids see
when they walk into our shelter.)*

Chapter 15

"Sister, am I going to heaven?"

June 1994

"I'm not afraid, Sister," Michelle said. "Really I'm not."

Her eyes had that look that the dying sometimes get ... a serene gaze that can seem close to angelic. That's how I knew she truly meant what she said.

I took her frail hand and pressed it to my heart.

She had lost so much weight, her hands were as light as birds' wings. I felt if I didn't hold on, they could just flutter away, towards heaven.

She smiled at me, a smile that could light up a room. That's what the rest of the kids at Covenant House remember about Michelle the most. She was always ready with a smile.

"Sister? Can I ask you a favor?"

"Ask away," I replied, my throat sore from holding back tears.

"Will you be with me when I die? Just like this, holding my hand?"

"You can count on it."

Michelle was already HIV positive when I met her.

That was back in 1990. She showed up at our door late one night — a scrawny, raven-haired beauty with deep-set eyes and an infectious laugh.

But the symptoms, those horrible symptoms of AIDS, had already begun to eat away at her....

Sometimes she had night sweats and cried out in her sleep. When she woke up in the morning, the sheets would be soaked all the way through.

She had a hacking cough that never left her. And there were dry patches on her skin that nothing could seem to cure.

We fed her and clothed her and loved her, just like we do all our kids. Only this time, it was a little different.

Because there was no escaping her fate. The kids knew it, I knew it, our staff knew it.

Sooner or later, Michelle was going to die.

There were so many things she wanted to know about death and dying — questions that have challenged theologians and philosophers since the beginning of time.

Questions that, often, I didn't quite know how to answer.

"Sister, why did God give me this disease?"

"Sister, does God accept drug addicts in heaven?"

"Sister, will I find someone to love me in heaven?"

The best I could do was tell Michelle what I believe: that God's love and forgiveness is limitless.

That when she left this earth, she would leave pain and suffering behind. That the unconditional love she never received from her parents would be found in the tender embrace of a loving God.

When I told her these things, she nodded sagely.

"You know, that's just how I thought it would be. That's why I'm not scared to die. I think heaven is going to be a wonderful place, where I never feel lonely or sad.

"You know what I think heaven will be like, Sister?"

"What?" I asked.

"Like living at Covenant House."

We buried Michelle just a few weeks ago. I wish you could have met her, and gotten to know her as we did. I think you would have liked her. I know you would have....

A lot of people condemn kids like Michelle for contracting the HIV virus. They think we should put them behind closed doors and pretend that they don't exist.

But that's just another way to reject them for doing what they have to do in order to survive.

Some contract HIV by prostituting themselves in order to buy their next meal. Others risk infection every time they get high. But they do it anyway.

Because that's the only way they can cope with the horror of life on the streets ... and the knowledge that they have been cast aside by the very people who were supposed to love them without judgment or reservation.

Well, there's one place they can come where they will never be cast aside. Michelle called it "heaven on earth."

The building's a little old and falling apart in places (some would say the same of its President!). But as long as both Covenant House and I are still standing, we will welcome every one of God's children with open arms.

If you had looked into Michelle's eyes and seen the light of hope and trust that shone there in her final days on earth, you would have welcomed her into your heart as well. I know you would.

Despite her suffering, Michelle never gave up hope. Before her last visit to the hospital, she was making plans to enter nursing school. After all she had been through, her fondest wish was to devote her life to helping others.

And I believe that she did just that.

You know, the kids put together her Memorial Service themselves.

They read poems by Maya Angelou and Karen Johnson. They told stories. And sang songs. One was by a singer named Eric Clapton. The kids tell me he wrote it right after the tragic death of his young son.

It's called "Tears in Heaven." We all cried when the kids sang it. You couldn't help but cry....

In 40 plus years, I've seen so many miracles. I've seen street kids that many believed were beyond redemption summon up the strength to deal with their pain — and make something beautiful of their lives.

But I'm not sure I've ever known anyone stronger than that tender-hearted girl who arrived on our doorstep four years ago ... and changed our lives forever.

I'm so grateful that Covenant House was here for Michelle. I spend a part of every day being thankful for the kids that God has sent to us (and even the ones He has taken back).

And I never ... we never ... forget the people like you, who make it all possible.

P.S. I know that, in some ways, this was a sad story. But here's the most encouraging thing I can say to you: that fact is, when Michelle had nowhere else to turn, we were here for her. She had a chance to know love and compassion for the first ... probably the only ... time in her life. That's the gift *you* gave to her.

Dear Sister Mary Rose,

I have just read your newsletter about Michelle and I know the terrible pain and suffering that poor girl felt during her time on this earth. I lived 12 years of my life being sexually abused and three years being passed on from foster home to foster home. I never lived with my mother until I was 16. I have always lived with my dad. I couldn't live with my mom, she didn't want me. So Mom took me to San Francisco. I was forcefully put in the car and was watched like a hawk. I was told that I was bad and I would go to Hell. I had no family. So, finally we reached San Fran. She said, "Here you are. Make it on your own kid. That's what you want. You got it. Bye." I was left on the streets of San Francisco, alone, scared and no place to stay. I went to a youth shelter for homeless and run-away kids. So, I know what those kids are going through. I've been there. I enjoy working with kids and want to become a pre-school teacher. I also want to help other kids. I want to help kids get off the streets, and just be their friend, be their big sister. I so much want to help. Can I?

B.M.

Epilogue

I don't think this book could have been written 10 years ago, or even five years back. The world we all live in — and particularly that dark, not-so-hidden-part-of-the-world that ensnares street kids — is changing too fast.

Viewed from a statistical perspective (and make no mistake about it, this is how the underworld views these kids, as in "he can 'do' $400 a night" ... "she's worth $2,000 a week to me" ...) you and I are staring full face into two huge 1994 realities.

The first? Simply stated, the number of street kids is growing. This year, more than 1,000,000 kids will end up on America's streets, a number that seemed unthinkable not too many years ago. Our country has always had street kids. But in today's America, an America continually beset by family units breaking down and breaking up, neighborhoods falling apart, and community clubs and associations deteriorating — the numbers of kids falling by the wayside is increasingly alarming.

Even worse, while the "supply" of new kids pouring out onto our streets is never-ending, the demands placed on them today are extraordinary. Sexual abuse ... physical abuse ... an increasingly expanding sex industry ... AIDS ... TB ... wanton violence — today's street kids face horrors that were unimaginable just a decade ago.

More than ever then, the race to rescue these kids is a race against the clock. Just a decade ago, we could still save a kid if we could reach him that first critical year on the street. Now? We must reach him or her those first few months, even weeks. Otherwise, it will simply be too late.

Every day, every hour, is that important.

I'm praying you will begin your first hour of helping our kids today.

Will you help me help them? Believe me, asking for help is not easy. Especially asking someone you've never met before. But these kids are very desperate. And your help today could mean so very much in their lives.

Please ... if it's possible, please help them today, if you can. Please. Thank you, and God bless you.

In God's love,
Sister Mary Rose McGeady
For the kids

Where do we go from here?

My newsletters tell an incredible story ... but they only tell part of the story. Wrapped around the letters I wrote to my friends, I've also included words written to me by others — poems and prayers written by our kids, and letters sent to me by donors who were moved by what they see happening in America today.

And almost every word in this book — whether they were penned by me, a runaway kid, a nervous grandmother, or a teenager in school — carries a consistent message: the American family is falling apart. And we must, each of us, do what we can to repair it. Now!

I passionately believe the breakdown of the family unit is the single deepest ethical and moral challenge of our generation. Whether we respond to it will depend on the resolve and willingness of all of us to commit ourselves to the care and protection of family life. The time for repairing endangered families and rescuing their children is not after they have fallen apart!

The question then is ... how? How can each of us make a difference in repairing the American family? And how can we begin to make that difference now?

Because the survival of the family is so very important to our futures, we have prepared a special Family Survival Guide which can be found on the following pages. This Guide features the best things we've learned over the years working with hundreds of thousands of kids, as well as good, time-tested values that we never let ourselves forget. We hope you will share these pages with a parent you know who may need help. Thank you!

Family
Survival
Guide

Reflections on
Raising Kids Today

Values — Teaching Them in Today's World.

Communicating your values has never been more important than it is today. And the good news is, it all begins and ends with you.

When all is said and done, parents have far more influence over instilling values in their kids than any other factor.

Here are some simple, and very important, things we should all remember about values, and passing them along:

- Kids get their sense of what's right and wrong from people they love and respect. No one has more influence over teaching values than you do. Your input can make all the difference!

- When it comes to teaching values .... action *always* speaks louder than words. Kids today have a "show me" mentality. They need to see the values lived out by you. Respect for life, respect for other people, honesty, integrity ... kids get those from watching you. The old saw has never been more true ... children *do* learn what they live!

- Families are still the best vehicle for raising children. A loving, nurturing family unit, of whatever form, creates the kind of environment kids need to learn what's right and wrong ... and how to love themselves, too. Values are best inculcated in an environment of love and acceptance.

- Always take time to sit and talk to your kids. Don't be afraid to say what you feel (but don't ever be too closed to listen to what your kids think).

- Always strive to teach your kids to love and respect themselves as children of God. A healthy love and respect for themselves is incredibly important for any kid. It's also the first essential step in helping a kid also learn a love and respect for those around him, and God.
- Nobody has said it better than Jesus. Those three words, "Love Thy Neighbor...." are an important message for every kid!

You've Got a Tough Job.

Most of us were never taught to be parents. So we can't help but disappoint ourselves sometimes. How often have you heard yourself using the very words you hated hearing from your own parents?

And when our kids become teenagers, it gets even harder. They seem to reject everything we've taught them. As far as they're concerned, we know nothing. Our values and beliefs are constantly challenged. Every word we utter is seen as interference. Emotions run high.

But we're more important to our teens than ever. As they try out the values of their peers, who are more influential than ever, we counter the pull of drugs and alcohol. These entangle children every day and can ruin their lives.

The Stakes Are High.

Teenagers who don't get what they need at home look elsewhere. Some run away from home. Many more consider other ways of running from pressure — a once bright and happy son escapes to drugs, a vivacious daughter starts drinking. Think about these facts:

- Each year, one million students drop out of high school or are chronically truant.
- Four out of 10 teenage girls will become pregnant before age 20.
- Although marijuana use has declined in the past years, addiction to cocaine, especially crack, has doubled.
- One in four teens develops a drinking problem during his teen years; about 10,000 will die in alcohol-related accidents this year.
- Each year, 5,000 to 6,000 teens die in suicide-related deaths, and the number is growing, one every 90 minutes. For every death, at least 100 other young people attempt suicide.

The Turbulent Teens.

Teens face many pressures that adults don't take seriously. Their bodies are changing — they have to adjust to the new person they see in the mirror. They feel different. They become interested in sex.

Self-doubt is constant. They feel pressure to conform and fear ridicule if they don't.

These changes can be bewildering, frightening and even depressing.

Teens can have remarkable insights. But they also surprise us with their lack of good judgment.

Your Teen Needs You.

At the time teenagers are crying out to be treated as adults, they also need a nurturing home, a refuge. And though they deny it passionately, they need structure, limits, lots of help sorting out their lives and most important, love.

In the turbulence of growing up, it is important for us parents to remember (even if our teens seem to forget) that we love each other. In the end, that's what makes the whole struggle worthwhile.

How Well Do You Know Your Kids?

You may say, "My teenager wouldn't do that." Most don't. But even if yours wouldn't, think about the following questions:

- Where is your child right now?
- What are your teen's deepest fears?
- Who is your son or daughter's best friend?
- Do your teen's friends feel welcome in your home?

Remember, a strong relationship with your children is the best way for you to guide them, and to prevent them from becoming a sorry statistic.

Getting Along With Your Teen.

Here are some ideas and techniques you can try to improve your relationship with your teen. If they don't work at first, keep trying. They take practice.

1. Make time for your teen. Find an activity you enjoy doing together and pursue it. If your invitations are declined, keep asking.

2. Listen, really listen. Because parents have so much to do and so little time, we often try to listen while cleaning, washing dishes or fixing the car. Put your chores aside so your teen knows you're really paying attention.

3. Take the long view. Don't treat minor mishaps as major catastrophes. Choose the important issues. Don't make your home a battleground.

4. Tolerate differences. View your teenager as an individual distinct from you. This doesn't mean you can't state your opinion if you disagree.

5. Respect your teenager's privacy. If a behavior is worrying you, speak up.

6. Let your teens sort things out themselves. Never say that you know how your teen feels. They believe their feelings (so new and personal) are unique. They'll learn otherwise — without your help. And never imply that their feelings don't matter or will change. Because teens live in the present, it doesn't matter that they'll soon feel differently.

7. Don't judge. State facts instead of opinions when you praise or criticize. Stating facts like "Your

poem made me smile," or "This report card is all
Cs and Ds!" leaves it up to your teen to draw the
appropriate conclusions. Teens are sensitive about
being judged — positively as well as negatively.

8. Be generous with praise. Praise your child's efforts,
   not just accomplishments. And don't comment on
   the person. "You're a great artist" is hard to live up
   to. "I loved that drawing" is a fact and comes from
   your heart.

9. Set reasonable limits. Teens need them. Your rules
   should be consistently applied — and rooted in
   your deepest beliefs and values.

10. Teach your teen to make sensible decisions and
    choices by encouraging independence and letting
    your teenager make mistakes. Don't step in unless
    you have to.

How to Make Anger Work.

All parents get furious at their children. We can't
help it. But some parents feel bad about being angry
and keep quiet. Though it's easy to say things in anger
that you don't mean, anger can also spark talks that
will help you and your teen get to know each other
better.

Some Guidelines.

- When you get mad, don't blame or accuse. Say
  how you *feel* — annoyed, irritated, upset, etc. —
  and why. Be specific. Talk facts. Blaming only

forces a teen to argue his point, arouses tempers, and kills dialogue.

- Think solution, not victory. Don't try to win arguments.
- Stick to the present incident. Fighting old battles will only aggravate a situation.
- Be careful not to attack your teen's person or character. Say, "I'm furious that you didn't clean up after the mess you made" — *not*, "You're a lazy slob!" Your son or daughter may give up trying to improve.
- If the situation is touchy, put your ideas in a letter. You can say exactly what you mean — and your teen will have time to think it over before answering.

Signs That Your Child Needs Outside Help.

- Suicidal talk of any kind. A suicidal teen may also give away valued possessions, make a will, talk about death or dying or say his family would be better off without him.
- Recent changes in sleeping or eating habits, thinking patterns, personality, friendships, study habits, activities. A sudden unexplained end to a long depression often precedes a suicide attempt. Major weight loss can be a sign of bulimia or anorexia — dangerous problems.
- Drug or alcohol use. You might notice: irrational or irresponsible behavior, lying, secretiveness, severe mood swings, a sudden increase in accidents. A

teen with a problem may have dilated pupils or wear sunglasses indoors, or complain about not sleeping or not feeling well. Valuables may disappear. You may find drug paraphernalia or alcohol containers around the house.

- A recent change in friends who you feel may be involved with drugs or alcohol may indicate that your child is involved or be a sign that your child is having other problems.
- Law-breaking behavior, even if the police and courts aren't involved. You might notice new possessions and money not accounted for.
- Poor self-image. Doubts are normal. But persistently low self-esteem is a problem.
- Serious depression. Listlessness, loneliness, withdrawal, difficulty making friends.
- Rebelliousness to the point of total, continual defiance.
- Problems at school, including class-cutting, absenteeism, a sudden drop in grades.
- Fears or anxieties that interfere with everyday activities.
- Problems between family members that aren't solved by listening and discussing. In fact, family changes such as a death, divorce or remarriage are times when teens often need some outside help.

When to Get Help For Yourself.

- Things aren't going well with your family but you can't figure out why.

- You disagree totally with positions your spouse has taken on issues concerning your teen and the two of you can't find a compromise.
- You have trouble holding a job.
- You are abusing drugs or alcohol.
- You get violent with your teenager and can't control yourself.
- Your spouse gets violent with you or your child.

What to Do If Your Teen Runs Away.

Most kids who run away return within 48 hours. Those who stay away can find themselves in many dangerous situations. So do everything you can to bring your child home.

- Keep a notebook recording steps you've taken and dates.
- Check in with: neighbors, relatives, and your teen's friends, teachers, employer or co-workers.
- Contact local hangouts and hospitals.
- Call the police. Have an officer come to your house to take a report and pick up recent photos, dental records and fingerprints if available. Get his name; badge number and phone number; the police report number; and the name of the officer who will follow up.
- Make sure the police lists your teen in the National Crime Information Center (NCIC) to the state clearinghouse on missing children, if there is one in your state.

- Contact the National Center for Missing and Exploited Children for help with law enforcement officials — 1-800-843-5678.
- Call the Covenant House NINELINE for support and to check for messages. Leave a message. Also check with any local runaway hotlines.
- Contact runaway shelters locally and in nearby states.
- Make posters with photos of your teen, listing: age, height, weight, hair and eye color, complexion, physical characteristics (such as scars, birthmarks, braces or pierced ears), circumstances of disappearance, your phone number and police contacts. Distribute these to truck stops, youth-oriented businesses, hospitals, law-enforcement agencies.
- Be prepared for the first conversation with your teen. Whether in person or by phone, show concern, not anger. Say, "I love you."
- Prepare to quickly begin resolving the problems which caused your child to leave home. When your child returns home, emotions are likely to run high. Someone outside your family can help you all deal with these emotions. You may find that planned time for your teen in a temporary residence or shelter is necessary while you are resolving problems. So get outside help from a trained counselor.

A Gift To Be Embraced

Reflections on the
Covenant House Faith Community

The following was written by Alec Aspinwall, a former member of the Covenant House Faith Community in New York City.

Even after making the decision to visit the Covenant House Faith Community in New York City, I have to admit I was still somewhat suspicious. The closer I got to the address on Eighth Avenue in the heart of Times Square, in fact, the more my questions grew. What would draw normal people away from their comfortable lifestyles to pray for three hours a day and work with street kids while making $12 a week? What was drawing me?

For some time I had been searching for a way to deepen my relationship with God, and there was certainly something pushing me to take a closer look. Now, that courage seemed foolish and even a little frightening as I stood on the doorstep waiting for someone to answer the bell. I tried to look nonchalant, but as I glanced across the street, my eyes read the invitation posted on the door of the porno theater and I turned away in disgust — but without success. All around me, as I looked to the left and then to the right, the sorry sights and sounds of a string of "adult entertainment centers" made my stomach turn. I felt stunned. Is this where I had to live if I wanted to feel closer to God? Was I crazy? The eyes of the street people told me what I already knew. "You don't belong here," they said. They were right. I didn't belong there.

Then the door opened, and I was met with a warm smile. I tried to contain my gratitude for the timely rescue.

Once inside I was surprised by the size of the dwelling. It consisted of two six-story buildings joined by a large chapel. The dormitory-style living was neither elegant nor impoverished, but quite plain. The people I was soon to meet, however, were anything but plain.

I found myself in the midst of a Christian "melting pot." There were nurses, teachers, nuns, businesspeople, laborers, retired mothers, and recent college graduates. They had come from all over the country and even from abroad. Although Catholic in prayer and worship, the Community also had members from various Christian denominations. There were conservatives and liberals, rich and not so rich, young and the young at heart. Each had a different story to tell as to why they had come to Covenant House, but their differences were united by the call to strengthen their relationship with one God. To do so, they were willing to accept the challenge of intense prayer (three hours a day), communal living, and working with the kids of

Covenant House, whose lifestyle on the street can make them pretty tough to deal with at times. They hurt so much that sometimes the only way they can feel better about themselves is to hurt you instead.

I had also expected Community members to be a solemn bunch, bearing the weight of the pervasive tragedy that surrounded them — but I found just the opposite to be true. The Community had a vibrant spirit that was full of life and laughter. Somehow the pain they were daily exposed to had actually made room for joy. I'm not saying that I didn't perceive their own suffering, for many of them shared with me the struggles they were experiencing with the kids of Covenant House and with themselves. But they were beginning to see their struggle no longer as a punishment to be endured, but as a gift to be embraced. I began to think that there might be something to that line from the Gospel about how "dying to yourself will bring new life."

By the end of the week, I had a lot to think and pray about. Was I ready to commit to a minimum of 13 months of three hours a day of prayer? Could I dedicate myself to a simple lifestyle in a chaste community? Was I able to let go of the stability offered by my loved ones and my career? Was I willing to be sent to any one of the Covenant House sites assigned to me and work at any job, whether it was working directly with the kids or not? Most of all, could I really love those hardened street kids and let myself be touched by their pain?

I went home to California and asked God to give me a sign. Something simple. An eclipse maybe! No sign came. What did come, finally, was a sense of peace that told me it was all right to go against all the norms and ambitions ingrained in me and take a step forward in faith. After receiving a letter from the Orientation Director, I gave notice at my job and began to make plans to come back to New York.

It's hard to believe I've been here a year now. I've learned so much about myself, the kids, and God. I've learned, for instance, that drawing closer to God is a constant challenge and process. Street kids, I've come to learn, really have soft centers underneath those hard exteriors, and they often have more to teach me than I them. And God is always there, even though sometimes I don't recognize Him.

I still don't like the neighborhood, and I still get the same stares on the street that I did a year ago. Only now, sometimes I see Christ behind the cold eyes, and He reassures me, "You do belong here."

If you would like more information about joining the Faith Community, please write to Orientation Director of Faith Community, 346 West 17th Street, New York, NY 10011-5002, or call (212) 727-4971.

Need help with your kids?

*Call our NINELINE counselors
at 1-800-999-9999.*

*We'll put you in touch with
people who can help you right
in your hometown.*

1-800-999-9999

This call is free.

Covenant House
346 West 17th Street
New York, NY 10011-5002

Covenant House Florida
733 Breakers Avenue
Fort Lauderdale, FL 33304-4196

Covenant House New Orleans
611 North Rampart Street
New Orleans, LA 70112-3540

Covenant House Alaska
609 F Street
Anchorage, AK 99501-3596

Covenant House California
1325 N. Western Avenue
Hollywood, CA 90027-5611

Covenant House Texas
1111 Lovett Boulevard
Houston, TX 77006-3898

Covenant House Donor Assistance Line: 1-800-388-3888

"I bound myself oath, I made a covenant with you ... and you became mine." **Ezekiel 16:8**

The only way to stop the pain and degradation of street children is to get more people involved in solutions to the devastating problems they face every night of their lives.

After you read this book, please pass it along to a friend. If you would like more copies, just fill out this coupon and return it to us in the envelope provided. And know that because you took the time to care, a kid won't have to sell himself to survive tonight.

Please send me _____ **copies of** *Am I Going to Heaven?* **To help defray the cost of sending you these books, we request a minimum donation of $5 per book.**

Name _____

Address _____

City _____**State** _____ **Zip**_____

Please make your check payable to Covenant House.
Your gift is tax deductible.

Many people like to charge their gift. If you would like to, please fill out the information below:

I prefer to charge my: _____**MasterCard** _____**Visa**

Account # _____

Amount_____ **Exp. Date** _____

Signature_____

Mail to: **Covenant House**
            JAF Box 2973
            New York, NY 10116-2973

COUPON

Or, call 1-800-388-3888 to charge your gift on your MasterCard® or Visa® or to get more information.

"I bound myself oath, I made a covenant with you ... and you became mine."　　　　　　　　　　　　　*Ezekiel 16:8*

Covenant House depends almost entirely on gifts from friends like you to help 31,000 homeless and runaway children every year. We provide food, clothing, shelter, medical attention, educational and vocational training, and counseling to kids with no place to go for help. Please help if you can.

YES! I want to help the kids at Covenant House.
Here is my gift of: ☐ **$10**　☐ **$20**　☐ **$25**　☐ **Other**

Name _____

Address _____

City _____ **State** _____ **Zip** _____

Please make your check payable to Covenant House.
Your gift is tax deductible.

Many people like to charge their gift. If you would like to, please fill out the information below:

I prefer to charge my: _____ **MasterCard** _____ **Visa**

Account # _____

Amount _____ **Exp. Date** _____

Signature _____

Mail to:　　**Covenant House**
　　　　　　　　JAF Box 2973
　　　　　　　　New York, NY 10116-2973

COUPON